STEPPING

UP

12 WAYS TO REV UP, REVITALIZE, OR RENEW YOUR CAREER

S. GARY SNODGRASS

GREENLEAF
BOOK GROUP PRESS

Austin, Texas

Published by Greenleaf Book Group Press
4425 S. Mo Pac Expwy., Suite 600, Longhorn Building, 3rd Floor,
Austin, Texas, 78735

Distributed by Greenleaf Book Group LP

For ordering information or special discounts for bulk purchases, please
contact Greenleaf Book Group LP at 4425 S. Mo Pac Expwy., Suite 600,
Longhorn Building, 3rd Floor, Austin, TX 78735, (512) 891-6100.

Design and composition by Greenleaf Book Group LP
Cover design by Greenleaf Book Group LP

Publisher's Cataloging-In-Publication Data
Snodgrass, S. Gary.
   Stepping up : 12 ways to rev up, revitalize, or renew your career /
S. Gary Snodgrass.-- 1st ed.
   p. ; cm.

   ISBN-13: 978-1-929774-41-8
   ISBN-10: 1-929774-41-9
1. Career development. 2. Success in business. I. Title. II. Title: Stepping up :
twelve ways to rev up, revitalize, or renew your career
HF5381 .S66 2006
650.14   2006934941

Printed in the United States of America on acid-free paper

06 07 08 09   10 9 8 7 6 5 4 3 2 1

First Edition

CONTENTS

Acknowledgments

THIS BOOK is dedicated to Patsy T. Snodgrass, my wife and partner.

I am also indebted to my parents, Lloyd and Jerry Snodgrass; to my brother, Steven L. Snodgrass, MD; to Harold E. (Hal) Pendexter Jr., mentor and friend; to Marilyn B. Tedesco, for her valuable assistance; to Cheryl Jefferson, for her early contributions; to all my past and present colleagues at Exelon Corporation and USG Corporation; and finally, to my children Patrick, Amy, and Matthew Snodgrass, with a special thanks to Amy for her editorial assistance.

Introduction

D O YOU WANT A fulfilling, exciting, high-potential career? Do you want your name to be synonymous with professional excellence and your work to be known for the highest standards of development and growth? If you do, and you're willing to step up and make those desires a reality, I invite you to read this book. "Stepping up" is committing yourself to advancing your education, your effectiveness, and your professionalism to reach the career goals you set for yourself, whether that means a corner-office management position or a successful start in a new profession. When you step up, you begin to associate yourself with excellence.

This book contains twelve guidelines that will lead you toward this level of achievement. Each three-guideline section concentrates on a key aspect of professional success. Section 1 will help you navigate the external business world, starting with the behaviors and attitudes that constitute your internal business environment. These behaviors and attitudes will guide you when circumstances change, provide perspective as you face challenges and seek opportunities, and promote a balanced work/life perspective.

To maximize these efforts, Section 2 stresses the importance of lifelong learning. Successful professionals learn something new each day. They choose to draw fresh insight and understanding from the turning points in their careers. Discover how to leverage such moments as educational opportunities and make your journey to success a joyful experience.

Making practical applications of what you've learned is equally important. Section 3 demonstrates how communicating your business strengths and personal brand can support your aspirations and solidify your focus.

Ultimately, this level of commitment can lead to the personal evolution discussed in Section 4. Through mentor relationships, tapping your full potential, and positioning yourself for the future by becoming a top performer now, you can recognize hidden opportunities, set new professional standards, and redefine success.

In short, by following the guidelines outlined in this book, you will rev-up, revitalize, and renew your career.

SECTION 1

THE BUSINESS ENVIRONMENT STARTS WITH YOU

THE BUSINESS ENVIRONMENT is both vast and intimate. It is vast in the sense that it offers unlimited possibilities. It is intimate because its progress is in individual hands—your hands.

Your daily perceptions, behaviors, and attitudes define how you navigate and shape the business world. Indeed, the business environment starts with you. Whenever you meet fresh challenges and seek different opportunities in line with your values, you create the means to succeed anew and bring a balanced perspective to your life.

SUCCEEDING IN A NEW ENVIRONMENT

ENVIRONMENTAL IMPACT is a term we associate with the natural world, but the savvy professional knows it applies to the business world as well. Each time some aspect of your business environment changes, your career is affected, and you need to reassess your strategies for success.

Part of a successful strategy is realizing that a change in your environment can take many forms. Accepting a position with a new employer or beginning a career in an altogether different field places you in a new environment that can initially be very demanding. You have to learn the names and roles of your new colleagues, master new skills, and function in rhythm with the way your new employer conducts business.

A lateral move or a promotion within your current organization also constitutes an environmental shift. Though environmental changes within an organization may be less disorienting than beginning a job at a new company or beginning a new career, they may require a similar adjustment period.

New environments are also formed in less obvious ways than changing companies or accepting a new position. The following are other examples of situations that constitute a new environment:

- You are assigned to another manager.
- The governmental regulations for your industry are revised.
- Your company acquires or is acquired by an outside organization.
- Your company incorporates technological advances.
- You win or lose accounts.
- Your chief executive officer develops a fresh philosophy.

In short, anything that impacts your organization or its management, customers, staff, or product has the potential to cause an environmental impact that alters your career.

Correctly assessing this altered landscape greatly improves your opportunities for success. As a first step, examine the new terrain and understand why it evolved. Then, probe more deeply by asking the following questions:

- How does my role now relate to the efforts of others?
- What are the service requirements of my position? To what extent have these changed?
- What are the gaps to address in this new environment?
- What are some of the more compelling challenges or problems to be solved?

Inquire about the experiences of your predecessor or ask colleagues in similar positions to share information about their experiences. What did they learn in similar situations? How did they measure their success? This knowledge will allow you to identify the skills you will need to succeed in the new environment.

Developing a measurement scale up front assists you in navigating uncharted territory, because it clarifies your destination and course. Another excellent method to help you get your bearings is to define what success meant in your former environment and what it means in your current situation. Seeing the distinctions will help you determine the changes you now need to make.

In addition, don't overlook input and guidance from your employer, colleagues, and customers as you measure your results. These individuals can ensure that you get a quick start when new environments evolve. They are the people who can answer your questions and aid you in understanding the changing culture, standards, and values. They can identify the shifts in decision-making channels, clarify how your new position is linked to the organization's mission and objectives, and define what you are expected to contribute.

You can further delineate the goals and expectations of your position by creating a job profile. Your job profile will help you clearly see where you are in your career, where you want to go, what you need to do, and how long it will take for you to reach your destination.

Writing Your Job Profile

1. Write a description of your current career, not only describing your position, but where you are in your internal and professional development.

2. Describe the achievements you envision over the next six months and in the coming year.

3. As you reach each milestone, compare your profile to your actual work experience.

4. Assess the growth and development needed to reach your near-term and longer-range goals and adjust your plans accordingly.

An evolving organization offers the best opportunities for innovation, change, and personal growth. This often makes it the ideal environment for intelligent risk taking, continuous learning, and volunteerism. You can contribute more successfully if you bring certain traits to this type of situation. First, inventory your skills and be persistent about filling in any knowledge gaps. Then you must strive to be flexible and creative. Keep in mind that once you've made a quick start, you want to keep the momentum going so you can continue to progress.

As you pursue this forward progression, be mindful of three key guiding principles: (1) Constantly increase your value by identifying and acting on the opportunities a change presents. Learn everything you can from the evolving situation, including new processes, skills, and contacts. (2) Learn about yourself. Decide what you want to be known for in the new environment and set an appropriate time frame in which to reinvent yourself. (3) Continuously evaluate what is and isn't working for you and the organization in this new situation, and adjust your development plans accordingly.

> **Case Study** *Anne Mulcahy climbed Xerox's corporate ladder steadily from the beginning of her career there in 1976 as a field sales representative. When the board of directors decided it was time to revamp how the company did business, it turned to Mulcahy. She visited Xerox employees around the world, raising morale and refocusing them on the company's future, not its past. She is now chairman of the board and CEO of Xerox Corporation, and considered by* Forbes *to be one of the most powerful women in the corporate world.* (John R. Schermerhorn Jr., James G. Hunt, and Richard N. Osborn, *Organizational Behavior* (Hoboken, NJ: John Wiley & Sons, Inc., 2005), 61.)

You can also take many practical steps to help you move forward in the midst of change. For instance, develop a relationship with a mentor; voluntarily undertake assignments for top managers; accompany a salesperson on her calls; offer to join a cross-functional or interdepartmental team; attend a seminar on a new topic; pursue lifelong learning to match new skills to evolving needs; consistently project a positive attitude; and be comfortable with change and ambiguity.

These actions, together with the previously outlined steps, will not only allow you to succeed in managing environmental impact, they will allow you to successfully impact your environment and, ultimately, bring your best to the ever-evolving business world.

Action Steps to Accelerate Your Movement into a New Environment

- During your first two weeks, get acquainted with four new people.
- In the first quarter, meet with your manager, compare your progress to your job profile, and discuss any adjustments you need to make.
- Complete a project in the first sixty days; then use the next thirty days to solicit feedback.

FACE CHALLENGES & SEEK NEW OPPORTUNITIES

I N WRITTEN CHINESE, the symbol for *opportunity* is identical to the symbol for *crisis*. Likewise, in business, opportunities often masquerade as challenges. Every problem, crisis, or mistake presents growth options to those who assess the situation with vision, position themselves strategically, seek responsibility, and move forward with conviction. Reaching this mindset is much like training for an athletic competition. It requires thoughtful preparation; a set of consistent, positive behaviors; and well-disciplined actions. The first step is recognizing an opportunity when you see one.

Frequently, opportunities are the result of change. As organizations shift to fit the evolving business world, corporate initiatives and priorities are realigned, which may affect every aspect of an organization, from its philosophy on down to how the receptionist answers the phone. Opportunities occur when you recognize and ally yourself with changes in your company's needs, values, culture, and daily operations.

In addition, perceiving that problems represent "progress in disguise" allows you to transform challenges into positive growth experiences. This is true regardless of your level in the organization. In fact, the people closest to the customers and those who are responsible for day-to-day operations often have the best opportunities.

Sometimes these situations are immediate, such as the daily opportunities for a customer service representative to positively influence the public perception of the company and build her reputation as a professional. Other opportunities are longer term, such as pursuing advanced education and the positions that become available with, for example, a master's degree.

Recognizing an opportunity usually requires knowledge beyond your company. By studying your industry and the global environment, you not only increase your knowledge, but the range of options available to you.

Once you identify an opportunity, there are several specific steps you should take to prepare to meet it. Begin by inventorying your skills and, where necessary, strengthening them. Constantly assess the value you deliver to your organization, especially as you master new work processes and acquire fresh knowledge. You should also be inquisitive and learn to spot emerging business trends. In addition, advise your manager of opportunities you're interested in, because many can occur within your current job responsibilities or department. New opportunities can arise in a variety of ways:

- Through visibility and credibility achieved in your current role
- Through exposure to others in the course of the typical scope of current business activities
- Through earning a reputation among colleagues as one who leads, delivers results, innovates, etc.

Since there is no way to know when or where an opportunity will come, it is best to always be prepared to make the most of your circumstances. The following is a list of steps that will help prepare you to seize an opportunity:

- Expand your network to increase your knowledge base.

- Enroll in professional or trade associations.

- Develop a relationship with a mentor.

- Offer to cross-train inside and outside your organization.

- Request special assignments or join a cross-functional team.

Together, these actions can prepare you to meet challenges and transform them into opportunities.

Once you're prepared, a consistent pattern of behavior will bring even more opportunities your way. As you participate in lifelong learning, each piece of knowledge you gain equips you to take on a broader range of responsibilities. For example, attending an evening workshop on future trends at a local community college can spark creative and innovative thinking about forward planning for business strategies.

Case Study *When Carly Fiorina took over as CEO of Hewlett-Packard, she faced the problem of leading a company known for a strong organizational culture but also facing major competitive pressures in a changing global economy. In her words, it was a company that was "so in love with its past" that "it had forgotten to build its future." But she saw HP's problems as opportunities for strategic change leadership. With confidence and hard work, she challenged*

> *old ways of thinking, dealt with resistance to change, and brought a new vision to the firm.* (John R. Schermerhorn Jr., James G. Hunt, and Richard N. Osborn, *Organizational Behavior* (Hoboken, NJ: John Wiley & Sons, Inc., 2005), 361.)

Likewise, if you regularly find something positive in the midst of adversity, you demonstrate you are a professional who is able to adapt and grow. If you jump at challenges when they arise, you'll be known as a take-charge person who can handle the pressure and deliver results.

Other behaviors will work in your favor, too, including persistence, intelligent risk taking, flexibility, taking responsibility for your actions and their consequences, taking initiative, finding fresh solutions, and finishing what you start. Build a reputation for excellence so that you are known as someone who creates value. Finally, be timely in your response, because many opportunities are fleeting, and you must act before they slip away.

Often this means you can't wait for direction but must take immediate action to derive the fullest benefit for you and your organization. If you do this with proper preparation and consistent performance, it will likely result in positive recognition.

By taking these steps and learning from challenges, you will become your company's competitive edge, its link to future opportunities and growth. You will also demonstrate that you are ready for additional responsibilities. Your confidence will increase, and you'll generate the momentum you need to move forward toward an exciting future.

If you don't see any opportunities in the pipeline, you must take action to create them from current short- and long-term challenges you observe.

Action Steps to Create Short-term Opportunities

- Question limits. Ask "what if" and offer to develop a pilot project to test the waters.

- Offer to chair a task force or focus group; coordinate a project, study, or implementation program.

- Consistently diffuse negative energy with a positive attitude and open-minded inquiry.

Action Steps to Create Longer-term Opportunities

- Volunteer for a special project, additional training, or a cross-functional assignment.

- Identify cultural limits and constraints, whether they are found in policies, procedures, or people, and then use positive persistence to expand boundaries and overcome barriers.

- Influence your organization to change, and accelerate the pace with innovative thinking and an expanded repertoire of ideas and solutions.

FIND A BALANCED PERSPECTIVE

A S A PROFESSIONAL in today's busy world, you don't want to perform a juggling act; you want to perform a balancing act. Why? Because work/life balance impacts every aspect of your existence, especially in the current business environment.

Today's business environment is one of increased employee, shareholder, and customer expectations; of rapid technological shifts; high-pressure market competition; a volatile economy; and the need to do more with less. Talent shortages, 24–7 demands on your time, multiple distractions, exhaustion, and intense pressure to succeed under near-impossible conditions compound the situation—and this is just par for the course.

To succeed in this arena, you must take a proactive stand on both your personal and professional responsibilities. In other words, you must balance competing priorities from all areas of your life. This whole life–whole person orientation is important because your competence and job satisfaction are impacted by factors far beyond the workplace.

> **Case Study** *Shelly Lazarus, chairman and CEO of the advertising firm Ogilvy & Mather, began as an account manager and then climbed through the ranks while raising three children. Lazarus sought out challenging, stimulating projects to maintain the passion and rewards she found in her work. Her advice to other parents who have demanding positions is to make sure they've found work that interests them. "You have to love what you're doing in your professional life. If you ever want to find balance, you have to love your work, because you're going to love your children, that's a given."* (Thomas J. Neff and James M. Citrin, *Lessons from the Top: The 50 Most Successful Business Leaders in America—And What You Can Learn from Them* (New York: Doubleday, 2001), 221.)

A drastic change in your home environment or the health of a family member can create conflicting priorities.

By planning for, recognizing, incorporating, and managing changes in crucial life areas, you can fulfill your needs and create a sense of balance that promotes personal and professional excellence every day.

In terms of your professional life, start by examining your goals. Where are you now? Where do you want to be? What will it take to get there? Remember that as you progress professionally, you will be asked to multitask at a higher level to meet the increasing demands of colleagues, shareholders, and customers, and to address complex business issues with clarity and insight. Such challenges are not for the faint of heart, which is why work/life balance requires you to address your heart both literally and figuratively.

Assessing the Balance in Your Life

1. Write descriptions of your work and life values.

2. Identify where they converge.

3. Identify where they conflict.

4. Use the points of convergence to describe your ideal, balanced life.

5. Examine the conflicts to discover how far you are from this ideal.

On the literal level, this may mean developing a personalized health and fitness regimen, addressing nutrition and sleep issues, and monitoring your stress levels. Figuratively, it means honoring your need for spiritual growth and change, and continually assessing the value of your work as it fits with the values of your life. Such an evaluation often leads to changes for the good.

Studies show that creating work/life balance can help you develop greater focus, increase your capacity for strategic thinking, enhance your resistance to stress, and provide the opportunity to exert a more positive influence on your organization's culture, not to mention on your own life and the lives of colleagues and friends. The following is a list of additional benefits that come with assessing your work/life balance:

- Clearer goals

- New, positive behaviors

- Forward momentum

- Fewer obstacles

- Healthier, more productive habits

- Enhanced leadership abilities

- Consistent personal and family behaviors and rituals

- Improved mentoring and relationship skills
- Improved management of adversity and change

In fact, your colleagues and your company will reap many rewards as you balance your work with your life. It is no secret that work/life balance positively impacts leadership abilities, productivity, goal attainment, and employee retention. Likewise, it fosters greater resiliency and gives companies the ability to cope with change.

Balancing your work with your life empowers you and your organization to make the best possible decisions. It enables you to focus on your core values, to bring them into alignment, and to cultivate the skills that will lead your company and help you, as an individual, design your tomorrow today.

Action Steps to Begin Balancing Your Work and Your Life

- For two or three months, keep a journal to compare your priorities to your use of time and clarify where you may need to make adjustments.
- Follow up with research, study, and discussions with your family and your manager as you consider a course of action to bring balance to your life.

- Develop a step-by-step action plan addressing the specific changes you want to make.
- Seek support for your change process through professional associations or your employee assistance program, or by taking a class, hiring a life coach, or taking a sabbatical.

SECTION 2

YOUR REAL PROFESSION IS LIFELONG LEARNING

A KEY PURPOSE OF EDUCATION is to help us discover our passions. Whether "school" takes the form of a university or a corporation, whether our teacher is a colleague or a friend, whether the curve is gradual or steep, one of life's great lessons is the importance of doing the work we love.

Lifelong learning can help us identify this passion and support us as we pass through all life's turning points. Education is also a measure of success, because for accomplished individuals, the learning never stops. Indeed, it is in the learning that we discover who we truly are and create professional lives that are a source of satisfaction and success.

NEVER STOP LEARNING

O F ALL THE TRENDS in professional development, few have as direct an impact on you as the way your organization selects, develops, and rewards its people. In times past, companies rewarded those who stuck it out through thick and thin. Now, organizations reward those who have unique knowledge and value-added perspectives. In other words, what you know increasingly determines what you are and what you become. Those who succeed commit to education as a lifelong process.

The benefits of continued learning can be measured in more than mere knowledge. Lifelong learning provides confidence, perspective, and the insight that makes you more effective, both in your current assignment and as a professional candidate for future endeavors.

Case Study *Leading and learning go hand in hand for Richard Branson, who cofounded Virgin Records and then went on to establish a variety of organizations under the Virgin brand. Branson's method of operation is to start a business, not buy it: "We start from scratch each time as a way of making sure it's really ours." Each new business requires hours and hours of research, which is okay by Branson: "I love to learn things I know little about."* (John R. Schermerhorn Jr., James G. Hunt, and Richard N. Osborn, *Organizational Behavior* (Hoboken, NJ: John Wiley & Sons, Inc., 2005), 296.)

To begin your climb up the learning curve, explore your interests and potential career direction. Answering the following questions will help you discover more about your career direction.

- What do I enjoy?
- Where would I like to spend the working part of my life?

- What activities are so fulfilling I would do them for free, as a volunteer?

- What do I want my professional legacy to be?

Determine what gaps exist between where you are now and where you'd like to be. For instance, do you need an advanced degree to switch professions or field experience to support your managerial desires? Whatever the case, review your strengths and weaknesses in terms of your skills and the requirements of your job. Then, seek validation. Talk to your peers, friends, or family about your assessment. Their feedback can ground you and aid in evaluating strengths and weaknesses you may not have considered.

Evaluate Your Strengths and Weaknesses

- Conduct research. Speak with human resources, contact professional associations, or interview people in your desired position to determine what skills and qualities are required.

- Determine which of your own strengths are transferable to the position you desire.

- Ask what education or experience you need to gain.

- Acknowledge any career/life conflicts. Are they reconcilable, and if so, how can you address them?

After you have evaluated your strengths and developmental needs, put together a game plan. Formulate a strategy that allows you to gain the experience you need to move ahead. Then, search for a teaching method that suits your learning style. If you seek workplace opportunities to lead a task force with colleagues from throughout the business, where in your community might you gain practical, hands-on experience? Could you lead a similarly comprehensive effort for a local nonprofit organization? Carefully consider how long your learning process will take and what resources you might need to tap and prepare accordingly. This may mean attending classes at night while keeping your full-time position, or perhaps saving for a few years before you take time off to focus on your studies.

Finally, stop planning and start acting. Take that first step, whether it's attending an open house, calling for a class schedule, or joining a workshop. Just do something to get up to speed, and be sure you enjoy the ride.

Remember, learning is a journey with many twists, turns, occasional detours, and side trips, each of which comes with unexpected challenges and opportunities. You will be successful traveling on this road if you commit to the educational process and stay the course for life.

Action Steps to Keep Learning for Life

- Take an Internet or virtual class, work with a peak-performance coach, or listen to books on tape as an alternative to taking a course in a classroom.

- Teach a class as a means of educating yourself as well as your students.

- Increase your knowledge by researching and writing an article for a professional journal, business textbook, corporate newsletter, or other publication.

EVALUATE YOUR CAREER TURNING POINTS

WHETHER YOU ARE HOLDING a steady course, trying to stay afloat on a sea of professional change, or feeling like you're going down for the third time, we all face turning points as we navigate our careers. Some turning points come in the form of opportunities such as a geographic move; others are associated with life events like marriage, birth, or death. Turning points can be forced upon us, as in the case of a promotion or layoff.

Often, however, a turning point will be less obvious. You may be disenchanted, or know in your gut that you're not having fun any longer in your current position, place of employment, or even career field. When you experience this sense of clarity, try to look at it as a valuable opportunity for recharting the course of your professional and personal life.

Each time you face a turning point, you know more about the world of work. Better yet, you know more about yourself and your priorities. This knowledge of who you are and what you want, coupled with your experience in work and in life, enables you to determine whether to continue on your current course, plot a slight change in direction, or move full steam ahead into something new. Even if a reorganization has made you feel as though your career is going south, a turning point can assist you in finding or recovering your "true north"—the work that excites you and gets your motor running.

This is the case even if you have smooth sailing now and for the foreseeable future. After all, if you don't assess where you're going, you'll be caught off guard if your career runs aground or you reach an unexpected destination. To avoid such disappointments, use turning points to study your career. If a turning point doesn't come along, schedule one, and then reevaluate to determine your next step. For example, choose a memorable date such as your birthday or the anniversary of your employment to evaluate your work situation. Remember, your career, like your life, is the sum of your choices. At each point, it's up to you whether you stay on board or jump ship. How do you know which way to go?

Case Study *John Mackey, founder and CEO of Whole Foods, began the empire as a small vegetarian business in his garage, where he sold food brought in by local farmers and bakers. When he decided to grow the business, he knew he would have to compromise and sell animal products. To balance his personal values with moving in a direction that was best for his business, he introduced humane animal-treatment standards. Mackey also placed a cap on executive compensation (no executive can earn in salary and bonus more than fourteen times what the average worker makes). Mackey's efforts have also helped make* organic *a household word.* (Amanda Griscom Little, "The Whole Foods Shebang," interview with John Mackey, *Grist Magazine*, December 17, 2004, http://www.grist.org/news/maindish/2004/12/17/little-mackey/.)

Start by assessing your priorities and trusting your instincts. Do your current industry, company, profession, and position still match your value system? If so, cultivate more of the same. If not, what has changed? Is it your business, or is it you? If you have the sinking feeling that your epitaph will read "world's hardiest commuter" instead of "maximized every moment," now is the time to make a change and get where you want to go.

Perhaps your destination is somewhere within your current industry, or maybe you love what you do but want your present job to be more satisfying. If so, assess your successes, skills, knowledge, and talents, and then identify the missing links between you and your goal of job satisfaction. If you're unsure of what you want, research a range of all interesting possibilities until you find a path you want to follow.

To move toward job satisfaction, consider these options:

- Moving vertically or laterally
- Enriching your current position by honing your expertise to a finer level
- Moving downward to a position that better suits your priorities
- Relocating to a different department, division, or city

If you learn, progress, and periodically reorient yourself to your "true north" throughout your career, it will be much easier for you to stay impassioned and enthused about your work. It will also broaden your options. This is especially true if you decide to change professions altogether. Begin this journey by figuring out what it is you love so much that you would do it for free (you should have determined this in Guideline 4). Next, write an assessment. Determine which skills carry over to your new field. Rest assured, many will! Knowing what you bring to the table is the great advantage of having experience in work and in life.

Change is challenging, but it is also a source of empowerment. If you are comfortable with change, you will have the courage to trade in your gold, silver, or bronze handcuffs for the opportunity to reignite your passion and fulfill your potential. Completing the following exercise will help you feel more at home with change.

- Make a list of the major personal and professional changes you've experienced.
- Evaluate which changes turned out successfully and which did not.
- What did the successful changes have in common?
- What did you learn from the less successful experiences?
- Combine these lessons to construct a fresh, positive approach to confronting change in your life.

Each step you take, no matter how small, can move you forward. And if you are inspired to embark on a brave new professional life, you don't have to face this life alone. You can take classes; network; go online; get or be a mentor, apprentice, or understudy; hire a life coach; volunteer; and more. Each of these interactions will encourage you to think outside of the box and use your turning point to turn a corner in your life and your career.

Whether you stay in your current position or not, a professional turning point is invaluable. If you remain, it can validate and reinforce your choices. If you move on, it can assist you in analyzing your situation honestly and inspire you to take advantage of opportunities. Either way, turning points empower you. They inspire a new commitment to meaningful work. Better yet, they move you from asking "What if?" to asking "What next?" so you can sail toward a better career.

Action Steps to Move You Forward

- Seek the broadest possible application for your skills and talents. Try idea-mapping exercises to extend this to its furthest level.

- Keep your career portable by applying big-picture thinking to your experiences and education.

- Change your expectations to match your new priorities. Use them to guide you as you continue your search.

GUIDELINE 6

MAKE THE ROAD TO SUCCESS A JOYRIDE

I F THERE'S ONE THING life experience teaches us, it's that the road to success is no longer straight and narrow. It turns, takes unexpected detours, or loops around full circle. Fortunately, each of these routes can lead to a fascinating destination, and the destination may not even matter as long as you're enjoying the ride.

But you'll only enjoy the ride if you take charge of your road from the driver's seat of your career. To steer in the right direction, you must practice personal career management.

Personal career management will help you drive toward more fulfilling work, better control of your time, increased salary and responsibility, or any other goal. Traveling in the direction of your true desires makes your career path more pleasurable. This style of journey benefits your employer, too, because it boosts morale, focuses priorities, increases productivity, and promotes a more realistic employment relationship.

One reality of commerce today is that companies must do more with less. Increased competition, globalization, accelerated technology, the economy, and world events leave an impact on careers at every level, resulting in leaner organizations populating the map.

In this environment, traditional internal promotion may be complemented by internal restaffing, but vacant positions may not always be staffed. As a result, there may be fewer upward moves employees can make. Fortunately, up is not the only direction there is to move. You can manage your career for success no matter what direction you're heading. There are many actions you can take that will accelerate your journey along the right course.

Start by assessing your strengths (see Guideline 3), which is critical to taking charge of your individual career management plan. Then learn to innovate, develop leadership abilities, increase your flexibility and productivity, and develop a global perspective. In addition, learn to live with ambiguity and to create new standards of professional success.

To increase your flexibility, try the following:

- Take a class or workshop unrelated to your current position and past experience. See what new ideas you can learn to apply to your life.

- Introduce variety into your routine—whether by changing the steps you traditionally apply to a project or altering your daily route to work.

- Swap jobs for a day to experience your organization from a different perspective.

Getting into the habit of learning constantly will help you enormously with efforts like these. Take classes to update your credentials, volunteer, and pursue lateral moves to broaden your horizons. Make your career portable with skills you can carry beyond your current position.

Case Study *Every day, the fifty Cistercian Sisters of Mount Saint Mary Abbey rise at three in the morning, pray until nearly eight, and then begin making chocolate—the enterprise they've chosen to help support their life of "beautiful simplicity." The eleventh-century order recently decided to move Trappistine Quality Candy into the twenty-first century with new desktop computers, a server, and an internal network. A Web ordering system and software system have* *streamlined the shipping process, while the new, faster, and more reliable computers have helped improve customer service. The end result is that the chocolate-making business is far more efficient—and far less of an intrusion on the nuns' peace and tranquility.* (Associated Press, "Nuns take to a sweeter, online order," *Daily Times*, April 21, 2003.)

You can also add value to your career by contributing more than you cost. You could do this by inventing a new product or creating a new service, identifying or spearheading a cost-saving initiative, or developing an enhanced revenue stream. Or you could try less traditional innovation, such as shaping legislation to establish a favorable business environment. Remember, it's your actions that make a difference, including the drive for personal excellence, which prepares you to take advantage of opportunities wherever they occur. Achieve personal excellence with the following:

- Superior job performance
- Outstanding productivity
- Rapid response time
- Good communication and interpersonal skills

In this context, many different kinds of moves may help you further your goals. A lateral move can allow you to expand your experience in a new position with a similar title. Other moves can give you the chance to grow in place and expand your current position by refining your expertise. You might also have the opportunity for a vertical move. Just remember, this is not always the best or only option. In fact, lateral, cross-functional, and nontraditional moves may allow you to grow into an opportunity rather than simply move up in a straight line. To nourish growth into possible opportunities, try the following:

- Be honest in your self-assessment and resolve any growth issues that impact your performance.

- Know your organization and yourself. Ask how you can work together more effectively.

- Define your professional strategy and career aspirations. Determine how these can best meet your organization's needs, and then communicate these thoughts clearly.

Occasionally, moving laterally will lead in an altogether different direction, toward another organization or profession. If this is where you're heading, explore what's available. Map out a plan, and take into account anything unexpected that you can think of that may surface along the way. If you get lost or hit a career pothole, slow down or stop for a moment and regroup. Consider what direction best suits your quality of life and what skills you need to speed you on your way.

Following these rules of the road will help your drive to success be a joyride and ensure you learn what you need to know to arrive where—and as who—you want to be.

Action Steps to Make the Road to Success a Joyride

- Review your career "owner's manual" and identify where your strengths lie to help you leverage passions to pursue and recognize areas to develop.

- Chart your journey by identifying and reflecting on key elements or points of interest.

- Become familiar with the road ahead, including any changes to anticipate and skill sets, such as technological abilities, needed to assure success.

Pack your bag and go for it! Just remember, don't burn any bridges or forget your way home.

Section 3

Communicating Your Self

COMMUNICATION IS THE BRIDGE between you and everyone you work with, including your peers, your staff, your manager, and your customers. To communicate effectively with others, though, you must know your wants and needs, your logical side and your emotional side, your professional goals and your personal values.

In other words, superb communication not only means communicating yourself—who you are—to others, it also means communicating between the many selves—spouse, parent, child, sibling, citizen, athlete, professional, you name it—that make you who you are.

REMEMBER THAT BUSINESS STRENGTHS ARE IN THE EYE OF THE BEHOLDER

WHEN YOU MOVE to a new business environment, remember that your strengths are in the eye of the beholder. Depending on the circumstances and other people's perceptions, characteristics that are an advantage in one situation may actually become liabilities in another. Disregarding this principle can give your career a "black eye" if your beholder doesn't like what he or she sees. For instance, if you move from a detailed, procedural position to one requiring flexibility and broader thinking, maintaining the first mindset may hinder your progress and, in the view of a new manager, can impair your success.

Such misjudgments occur because we lead with our strengths. We apply behaviors that have worked well in the past, and even if the situation is now radically different, we may assume the same approach will work again. Unfortunately, success is not guaranteed. In fact, your strengths might actually cause you to fail, especially if they were developed at the expense of other qualities that you now sorely need but haven't yet acquired. The solution is to evaluate the new circumstances and reformulate your strengths accordingly.

Start by assessing the past compared to the present. For instance, ask yourself if the analytical nature that was so valued in your former position might now be viewed as nitpicking; if your risk-taking tendencies make you appear like too much of a gambler for your new organization; or if your openness to suggestions makes you seem indecisive. The point of such self-examination is this: If you apply characteristics that were strengths in one situation without evaluating their suitability for another, you run the risk that they'll be seen as glaringly inappropriate.

To evaluate the new situation, create an information grid.

1. Across the top of your grid, write "Old Situation," "New Situation," "What's Now Needed to Succeed."

2. Down the side, list "Corporate Philosophy," "Reporting Relationships," "Business Objective," "Budget," "Cultural Considerations," and other pertinent categories.

3. In the boxes, describe each category in terms of the old and new circumstances, then compare.

4. Analyze what has changed, what has stayed the same, and where you must make adaptations for what's now needed to succeed.

Does this mean you must abandon past behaviors that have always served you well? Not necessarily. Instead, modify your approach. Identify gaps in your repertoire and fill them in with complementary strengths. For example, look at the people with whom you work. Appropriate interpersonal skills are highly valued in every business environment. If you're an individualist in a communal setting, you may need to develop better listening skills and a sense of reciprocity in order to succeed. Likewise, if you're a people person and find yourself in a more formal situation, a greater sense of reserve could provide a major advantage.

Case Study *Chairman, president, and CEO of Washington Mutual (WaMu) Kerry Killinger has challenged the concept*

of traditional retail banking with his "category killer" of cus-
tomer banking. Killinger has transformed the stuffiness and
blandness of the traditional bank into a laid-back atmo-
sphere that is more in line with that found in a coffee shop.
Associates (not tellers) wear blue shirts and khakis. Gone
are the velvet ropes and teller windows. Customers' children
play Nintendo in the WaMu Kid's Corner. With the WaMu
attitude—"helpful, sincere, at times irreverent"—Killinger
has turned a casual, customer-driven atmosphere into a
brand identity and a competitive advantage. (Stanley Holmes,
"The Wal-Mart of Consumer Finance?" *BusinessWeek*, March 21, 2003, busi-
nessweek.com/bwdaily/dnflash/mar2003/nf20030321_1093_db035.htm.)

Another area you may need to reevaluate is your
communication style. For instance, is your characteristic
self-confidence read as arrogance by your new peers? Is
the helpfulness your former colleagues valued seen as
smothering by your new staff? Either way, there are things
you can do to improve the situation, such as reading up on
communications skills, getting input on how others perceive
you, or hiring a management coach.

Examine other areas where your strengths may be per-
ceived as weaknesses, too. In each case, ask yourself some
pointed questions, such as if your sense of egalitarianism is

disrespectful in a more hierarchical environment or if your big-picture thinking obscures the small but significant.

Examine these common areas where strengths may be seen as weaknesses, depending on the corporate culture:

- Relationships to authority
- Patterns of strategic and operational thinking
- Approach to teamwork
- Style with customers or clients

An excellent way to begin the process is with an overall review of your unique characteristics and an assessment of whether, in your current situation, they are strengths, weaknesses, or both. To start, make a list of your individual qualities. Then, seek feedback from peers and your manager. To get feedback on your strengths and weaknesses, ask the following questions:

- "What is our organization's most important goal?"
- "What qualities are most critical to supporting this effort?"
- "Which of these qualities do I possess? Which do I lack?"
- "How can I acquire those I need and reinvent those I have to best serve the new needs of the organization?"

Next, use personal assessment tools and skills inventories to evaluate your characteristics, their impact, and any modifications that may be required. Consider working with a career counselor, management coach, or behavioral psychologist to reformulate your strengths.

Finally, determine what new skills you need, then acquire them by practicing lifelong learning. The entire process of fitting your strengths to your job will be more effective if you stay flexible to ensure continued growth and success.

By taking these steps, your repertoire of strengths will soon be apparent to any beholder, and you will not only become a success in their eyes, but in your own as well.

Action Steps to Reformulate Your Strengths

- Sharpen your CQ—your culture quotient—by more keenly observing beyond what the work is to how people are working with one another.

- Visit with colleagues from other organizations to understand cultural similarities and differences.

- Check to ensure that your signals to others, such as your relationship style and your appearance, are consistent with the image you wish to convey.

REACH THE NEXT LEVEL BY CREATING BRAND YOU!

REACHING THE NEXT PROFESSIONAL LEVEL may mean looking at things a bit differently, especially in the early stages of your career. To break through, you may need to try viewing yourself as a brand. Branding is an organized way of reaching your audience, that is, those who have the power to impact your position and provide you with opportunities. It's a highly effective method for communicating your desire and promoting your readiness to move ahead.

To begin the branding process, first take a close look at your "products." What are your core competencies and present reputation? How do others perceive you and your present and future potential, and on what basis? How do you perceive yourself? Do you need to reinventory your skills or make a few adjustments? If so, don't be discouraged. Brands are built over time. In fact, they are built up or torn down by everything you do, from passing on a meeting to the way you pass someone in the hall.

This constant flux is inevitable because a brand represents an emotional bond. It is the feeling people associate with you based on their interactions with you and what they have learned about you through formal and informal observations.

The following elements have an impact on your brand identity:

- Corporate culture
- Business beliefs and philosophy
- Your communication style and personal image
- What you have achieved and how

For instance, does your company value team players and discourage mavericks? Which type do your colleagues associate with you? Are you known for quality work, quick turnaround, finely honed skills, and helpful insights? What is your professional signature? In other words, what lasting impression do you make in your workplace?

One individual, a corporate writer, established a reputation for outstanding creativity and coming in ahead of schedule. Similarly, a young executive proved himself as a troubleshooter whose specialty was turning around worst-case scenarios. Both took the time to formulate a consistent brand identity that allowed them to get ahead. The key word here is consistency. Although your brand is established over time, remember that people make judgments quickly. This is why it's to your advantage to constantly excel and make those with the power to promote feel confident about promoting you.

Case Study *Earl G. Graves Sr. is known for believing that anything is possible. He is the president and CEO of* Black Enterprise *magazine, which he founded in 1970 to encourage business entrepreneurship among African Americans.*

His words of advice include the importance of believing in yourself and having a positive attitude. "If you tell someone you're going to do something, do it," says Graves, adding, "You have to live by your word." (John R. Schermerhorn Jr., James G. Hunt, and Richard N. Osborn, *Organizational Behavior* (Hoboken, NJ: John Wiley & Sons, Inc., 2005), 3; "Earl Graves," biography, *The History-Makers*, thehistorymakers.com/biography/.)

Targeting this audience is a key part of your breakthrough brand strategy. You may be communicating with an audience of one—your boss—or perhaps your efforts are directed at a larger group. It all depends on what position you're seeking. If your target audience is broad, consider what the members have in common, such as technology, creativity, or profit motive. Put yourself in their shoes to more accurately define your desired role. Remember, people will accept things that complement their prior experience with you, and this is where excellent performance comes in.

Excellence increases your brand portability and chances of breaking through. This is true whether your career is vertical and defined by industry, or horizontal and defined by activity. Either way, you can reach the next level by creating a brand that is sustainable and outstanding. You can also get there by being first.

Being first in any innovation, whether it means you're the first of your colleagues to seek out more advanced training or that you find the tweak that finally makes the customer-service program run smoothly, has multiple benefits. Consider the following:

- It establishes your leadership potential.
- It makes you look more promotable.
- It makes your brand the benchmark.
- It affirms your value in your audience's minds.

- It conveys your experience.
- It enhances your credibility.
- It attracts those interested in your talents.

Being first defines you in terms of value—that is, the benefits to the business associated with your efforts—instead of price, and increases your opportunities.

Another method of increasing your opportunities is to know what you need to do next to move ahead. Whether you require a vocal coach to polish your presentation style or want greater visibility through conference appearances, seek expert assistance. As you make these improvements, constantly update your résumé or portfolio. Make sure your mentors and professional cheerleaders know about your efforts.

Promote your new brand upgrades. Present them in terms of what needs to be done in your field—just remember to be consistent with your brand. If it helps, create a brand motto, a phrase that captures your identity, purpose, and value.

Stay with your vision, but adjust the steps you take to reach your goals as needed. This not only increases your effectiveness, it also gives your career greater longevity.

Finally, be selective. Actively choose your brand identity, then craft the professional signature that gives you the best opportunity to move ahead. You'll find clues to what you're looking for in your audience's behavior and expectations. Simply focus on your audience's perspective, and you will greatly increase your margin of success.

Action Steps to Creating Brand You

- Associate yourself with quality to give your career staying power.

- Know your own unique talents and continue to develop them through lifelong learning.

- Communicate your brand clearly and consistently. Linking yourself to one powerful idea will enable you to break through faster than anything else.

- Focus on your specific audience and be decisive, declarative, and definite in what you stand for. Don't try to be everything to everyone.

BE FOCUSED IN AN UNCLEAR WORLD

MANY PROFESSIONALS develop twenty-twenty vision after they see an opportunity pass them by. While you can always benefit from past experiences, be careful not to develop hindsight bias—that is, the tendency to connect past events to new circumstances in which they may not apply. However, it's important to try a new approach when the path you've been taking doesn't seem to lead anywhere. Try starting with a clean slate to focus on the future you want to create.

Developing this focus means selecting a goal and embarking on the steps toward its achievement. To choose your goal, examine your priorities and most pressing needs, and then revisit your ambitions and professional dreams. Decide what is most doable and desirable. Be sure to also examine your personal responsibilities to avoid conflicts. As your ideas develop, put them in writing, and then refine the list until you isolate the major goal that commands your attention.

Once this goal emerges, break it down into steps. Determine what part of the goal it makes sense to tackle first, whether it's doing research, speaking with your manager, or taking a class. After you've identified this initial step, organize your efforts. For instance, if you want a management job in your organization but your company requires an advanced degree, the education (plus an excellent effort in your current position) should be your primary focus.

Organize Your Goals and Focus on Achieving Them

- Identify which are short-, mid-, and long-term goals.

- Assess which goals are complementary and can be addressed simultaneously.

- Develop timelines for the goals you want to achieve.

- Support your efforts by learning skills to enhance your ability to focus, such as speed-reading, reflection, effective listening, tuning out distractions, and critical thinking.

One way to start focusing is by identifying those who have traveled a similar path and asking them for insights on how to begin. You might also take a class, work with a mentor or coach, volunteer for a new assignment, or join a committee or professional association to develop your insights and examine your goal from every possible perspective. It is also crucial that you communicate your focus to yourself and others on a regular basis.

Case Study *Gary Talbot was paralyzed from the waist down in an automobile accident in 1980, but even after the accident, he continued his love affair with cars. After years running his own mechanic shop despite recurring health problems, he earned a degree in mechanical engineering and started work at the General Motors Mobility Center. Talbot and his team are changing the way the automotive industry looks at designing vehicles for the disabled. He now works with executives who are spearheading the design of future vehicles that will address the concerns of the disabled and elderly during the earliest stages of design.* (Richard S. Chang, "He's Driven to Help Others," *Parade*, June 28, 2006, http://www.parade.com/articles/editions/2004/edition_04-18-2004/featured_1.)

Specific, regular communication helps clarify your goal to those who can aid in its achievement. In other words, building public awareness often leads to opportunities because it puts you top-of-mind with those who can assist. Likewise, by refining your goal, you increase the depth of your commitment and your ability to accurately assess the various possibilities that cross your path.

As you make these assessments, remember to keep your eyes on the prize; remain consistent in the drive toward your goal. To assist with this effort, create a personal support group or join a professional association with a focus that matches your own. Once you have such a support system, make sure to stay in touch.

Communicate with Your Support Network

- Hold regular meetings to discuss your progress.
- Give a presentation or workshop showcasing your new knowledge.
- Write an article for your organization's newsletter based on what you've learned.
- Promote yourself as a new go-to person and the in-house expert.

- Be attentive to your manager and colleagues. Your achievements will affect them first. Be open to your colleagues' ideas, not defensive—let them influence you.

Another highly effective action is to keep a progress log. Use the log on a daily basis to record the steps you've taken toward achieving your goal. With long-term goals in particular, the progress log can confirm that you are growing, learning, and moving ahead.

The log can also show you if you're diverting from your path or experiencing down time. If either is the case, reassess the situation to learn why your focus has changed. It may be that you need to correct your direction, develop a new goal, or perhaps simply recommit to your original ambition or seek reinforcement from your support network. This type of communication is especially important if you've already reached your goal and are ready to focus on another, higher-level ambition.

Focus can accelerate your achievements and sustain you over the long haul, whether it's graduate school or your climb up the ladder of success. In any case, the ability to focus gives you foresight and clarity as you move toward the future, because in business, as in life, what you focus on is what comes to pass.

Action Steps to Avoid Hindsight Bias

- Compare your level of experience in a former situation to your level of experience now.

- How have you changed? What have you learned since that earlier incident?

- Write a description of how the old you would handle a situation, then how the new you would handle it. Compare your results. Remember, to get a different outcome, you need to try a different approach.

SECTION 4

PERSONAL EVOLUTION: WHEN YOU'RE READY TO STEP UP

THE BEST WAY to demonstrate that you are ready to step up in your career is to become a symbol of excellence to yourself and others. An excellent performance allows you to position yourself for stardom and to accelerate your breakthrough to the next level. It also gives you the confidence you need to continuously rev up, readjust, or even reinvent your career.

This excellence can evolve further every day. Each project, communication, business interaction, and mentoring experience in which you are involved is an opportunity to develop as a person and a professional. Indeed, excellence, more than any other quality, is the way to show the world you're stepping up.

EFFECTIVE MENTORING BEGINS WITH "WE," NOT "ME"

A**LTHOUGH THE WORD** mentor begins with "me," it is not a me-first process. It's a we-first process. Mentoring is a relationship between two individuals who want to benefit from a professional exchange and who are both willing to share. What they share may be a specific agenda designed to help one or both develop skills and realize potential, or it may be a more free-flowing discussion of career knowledge, political observations, cultural considerations, long- or short-term goals, and other exploratory topics. In fact, exploration is one powerful advantage of having a mentor.

A mentoring relationship provides you with a protected, confidential environment where you can experiment, learn, and grow. It offers a supportive, action-oriented atmosphere in which you can take chances, ask questions, analyze mistakes, and celebrate triumphs. It is also an opportunity to improve yourself, to refine and take ownership of your professional development, and at some point in your career, to become a mentor to someone else. Participating in such a relationship primes you to evolve. This evolution not only benefits you, the mentee, but your mentor and your organization as well.

Indeed, today's global economy demands a more diversified workforce. Successful organizations know this means employees must be trained and nurtured at every level. Mentoring is an effective way to accomplish this goal. In addition, it increases quality and productivity, promotes recruitment and retention, creates a broader exchange of information, fine-tunes professional skills, and provides a support system that encourages employees to succeed.

Case Study *Southwest Airlines president and CEO Colleen Barrett believes success begins with a leadership* *commitment to all employees. She says the firm has three types of customers: employees, passengers, and shareholders. Barrett says defining employees as customers serves an important purpose: "If senior leaders regularly communicate with employees, if we're truthful and factual, if we show them that we care, and we do our best to respond to their needs, they'll feel good about their work environment and they'll be better at serving the passenger." Everyone is expected to be great at "TLC"—tender loving care for employees and customers. "We tell job applicants we're in the customer service business," says Barrett. "We just happen to provide airline transportation." Southwest provides abundant leadership classes and seminars, outside speakers, meetings with senior managers, roundtable discussions, and brown-bag meetings with employees. Barrett describes herself as a mentor, willing to work with "anyone who seems to have a passion for what he or she does, or who has a desire to learn."* (John R. Schermerhorn Jr., James G. Hunt, and Richard N. Osborn, *Organizational Behavior* (Hoboken, NJ: John Wiley & Sons, Inc., 2005), 27.)

Effective mentors have not only professional insight but emotional intelligence, good communication skills, and the courage to challenge assumptions. They also have a commitment to the organization and raise the bar to aid you in realizing your full potential. In addition, they participate in lifelong learning by taking advantage of the opportunity to learn from you, just as you learn from them.

This two-way exchange is the very foundation of a good mentoring relationship. Other necessities include shared interests, mutual respect, trust, confidentiality, honest feedback, and empathetic listening skills. Depending on your situation, you may also seek a mentor who is experienced in your area of expertise, or if you want a broader or different perspective, someone from outside your field. Keep in mind that a mentor can be found at any level. She may be a senior executive, a peer, or even someone junior to you from whom you can learn something specific.

As a mentee, there are several steps you can take to ensure that your mentoring relationship is productive and satisfying:

- Commit to change, and remember that the agenda is yours.
- Have a defined goal for the relationship, and communicate it clearly.
- Set parameters for which aspects of your career and life may and may not be discussed.
- Establish a mutually agreeable schedule, and set a predetermined length of time for the relationship.

- Choose an appropriate medium of communication, whether it's face-to-face meetings, conference calls, or e-mail.

- Set an agenda for each meeting.

- Establish a system for following up and evaluation.

- Give something back to your mentor, so that she can learn from you.

How do you find a mentor? There are many ways. To start, ask your manager if your company has a mentoring program in place, and if so, how it works. On a more informal level, you can identify who is chairing various committees or spearheading projects of special interest to you, take a class from or with an executive to see if you like his style, or volunteer for special assignments or interdepartmental task forces that will bring you in contact with potential mentors in other areas of your organization. Once you locate a promising candidate, speak with your manager about making appropriate contact to determine if the interest is shared.

You can also learn about potential mentors through the following sources:

- Your company newsletter or annual report
- Professional associations

- Volunteer organizations or activities
- Social venues

Don't be surprised if, as you grow and progress, you require different mentors at various stages of your career. You also shouldn't be surprised when potential mentees start coming to you. As you develop, your experience, perspective, and reputation will grow, and without doubt, so will your desire to reciprocate by sharing knowledge, insight, and all the lessons you learned from your own mentors. In fact, it is a sure sign that your personal evolution has reached a higher level when you become the "we" to someone else's "me" in the mentoring process.

Action Steps Toward Discovering a Potential Mentor

- Ask, "What is your teaching style?"
- Ask, "What is your business philosophy and attitude toward change?"
- Ask, "What are your most significant accomplishments, and how do you measure them?"
- Ask, "What can I do for you?"

ACHIEVE CAREER TURNAROUND BY TAPPING YOUR FULL POTENTIAL

DO YOU, like many established professionals, have an intense desire to apply new skills, or maybe even an overwhelming urge to shift careers? If so, this doesn't necessarily mean you're in the wrong field. Rather, you may simply need to introduce your interests to each other and see how they can partner in a more fulfilling way. Partnership among all your talents brings maximum creative excitement to your career and your life. Indeed, tapping your full potential can enrich your current position; aid your evolution toward a new, more satisfying vocation; increase your overall joy and balance; and benefit you in countless ways.

The process begins with identifying your passions. Ask yourself how much you love what you do and to what extent your work makes the most of your skills. Next, decide how challenged and excited you feel. Do you identify with the product or service you provide? Finally, assess whether your work relationships are creative and fulfilling. As you go through this process, unleash your imagination. What passions and interests do you have "in storage" that could complement your position and energize your career?

If you can't identify these passions, undertake a search. Do a skills inventory, visit with a career counselor, research online or at the library to become reacquainted with what you love. As a professional, you are ultimately responsible for creating this environment, the one in which you'll truly thrive. Fortunately, there are many ways to bring it about.

To focus your passions, work should do the following:

- Fulfill you
- Develop your natural skills
- Support you in the pursuit of your goals
- Reflect the values you consider authentic

For example, Steven L. Snodgrass, MD, a Kentucky surgeon, is widely recognized for his skill, but because his creative side needs another outlet, he now writes medical thrillers as well (*Lethal Dose*, 1996). Likewise, a PhD physicist in the Southwest indulges his love for botany by running an exotic plant business on the side. One young Chicago entrepreneur with a successful executive search firm indulges his passion by composing music and flying to the West Coast for weekend recording sessions. How can you develop your varied talents?

Case Study *When devoted environmentalist Roxanna Quimby, an artist and divorced mother living without electricity in the Maine woods, teamed up with Burt Shavitz in 1984 to begin selling items made from beeswax, she had no idea the company, Burt's Bees, would become a leading natural personal care brand.* (Susan Donovan, "First Person: Roxanne Quimby," interview, Inc.com, www.inc.com/magazine/20040101/howi-didit.html.)

There are many options. If you enjoy your current position but want to pursue a totally different passion, you can do it on evenings or weekends. Consider volunteering, attending class, taking a sabbatical, applying for fellowships and grants, or taking a transition job. For instance, after being laid off, one executive-level benefits manager took a position as a teaching assistant in a school for the severely disabled. This allowed the executive to explore a field that had always interested her before committing to a 180-degree career turn.

What all these individuals have in common is a desire to learn and do more, to shape and enrich their lives. To do likewise, you must overcome your fears and inertia. Focus on the rejuvenation engaging your passions can supply. To overcome the fear of career change, take these steps:

- Create a list of life categories that a career change will affect, such as finances, family, and schedules.

- For each category, list the best and worst things that could happen if your career change materializes.

- How realistic are the worst-case scenarios? What interim steps can you take to prevent them and begin your new career unburdened? With finances, for instance, can you adjust your budget? With your schedule, could you take individual classes instead of going to school full-time while pursuing a degree? Explore the options.

- Measure your concerns against the best possible outcomes to reduce your fears and focus on the future.

- Start envisioning the future today. To do this, try writing two versions of your autobiography, one version based on your life as it is now and one based on your life as if you were following your true passions. Compare and contrast the stories, then assess what you need to do to bring your life into alignment.

As you uncover your talents and fulfill your potential, your perspective will become more balanced. Your determination will strengthen and your life will be enriched. Best of all, making this effort will reintroduce you to your best, most authentic self.

Action Steps to Help Tap Your Potential

- Create a timeline for the rest of your work life. How have you spent the time up to now? How do you want to spend the work time that remains?
- Write your career epitaph. How do you want your work to be remembered?
- Ask a friend or colleague to write your career epitaph, and consider any insights about your potential and impact that arise from another's perspective.

POSITIONING FOR FUTURE STARDOM BY BECOMING A TOP PERFORMER NOW

T HE MOST LOGICAL WAY to predict your future is to create it, so if you aspire to a future as a business star, start by becoming a top performer now. Companies today need an uninterrupted flow of ideas, abilities, energy, and commitment. They are drawn to those who stand out from the crowd, who use up-to-date skills and leadership competencies to produce measurable results. Indeed, organizations actively seek such people. Does this sound like a star search? It is, and here's why.

The world business stage has changed dramatically. Companies have gone global, technology has exploded, and competition is fiercer than ever before. Traditional advantages, such as branding and lower costs, are no longer enough to ensure an organization's strength, let alone its survival. This is why the new competitive advantage is people—people with electrifying ideas and the ability to drive for outstanding results. It is also why entitlement is long gone, and there's no more security in the status quo. In fact, now there's only one status, and that's status go!

Status go is about enhanced employability, personal accountability, and operating at an exceptional level. It's about becoming a great employee and a rising star. Your outstanding performance now is an audition for your future position. Surprisingly few people understand this, but if you do, you're ahead of the game. In fact, if you are the top of the top performers, you may be considered a high-potential employee (HI-PO).

HI-POs go beyond great performance. They are seen as employees who can handle responsibilities one and two levels above their current positions. Some organizations even specifically label some employees "High Potential." How is such a person defined?

You know a HI-PO by his or her actions. She's the copywriter who foresees a problem, suggests an action, positively influences decision makers, and creates a new solution. She not only acts as a writer, but she also goes the extra mile to function as instigator, advocate, reporter, editor, and all-around communications expert.

> **Case Study** *Notre Dame's Father Theodore Hesburgh, president of the university for thirty-five years and now president emeritus, is considered one of the most influential figures in higher education in the twentieth century. With a dedication to leading with a vision, Father Hesburgh set out to redefine "the nature and mission of the contemporary Catholic university." During his tenure as president, Father Hesburgh raised Notre Dame's budget by $165 million and the endowment by more than $340 million, while also improving the quality of the faculty and the academic level of students.* (University of Notre Dame website, "Rev. Theodore M. Hesburgh, C.S.C.," biography of former president, http://newsinfo.nd.edu/content.cfm?topicid=12044.)

Another example of a HI-PO is the manager who constantly takes classes, brings fresh concepts to the table, and puts them into action. He not only shares what he's learned with the staff, but he also ensures that the staff has the opportunity to use its richest talents.

A HI-PO is the inventory professional who gladly drives two hundred miles in the dead of night to guarantee that a part is on hand for a customer the next day. HI-POs' stories are extraordinary, and so is their behavior.

You can follow suit. Regardless of whether your organization has a High Potential category, you can begin to position yourself now through your exceptional performance.

Start by delivering more than you promise, and consistently outperform yourself. You should also exceed expectations on a regular basis, seek more responsibility, value teamwork and diversity, provide leadership, and develop characteristics that allow you to go beyond the call of duty. In addition, learn how to communicate effectively and network. You must also assume some personal risk by thinking outside the box and exploring bold new solutions to business challenges.

Exceed the call of duty and become a top performer:

- Learn to be resourceful.

- Increase your level of comfort with ambiguity.

- Be open to saying, "I don't know but I'll find out."

- Take initiative and persevere until you reach quantifiable results.

When is the best time to assume these risks and begin your career as a high performer? Now! Though you may feel like you're walking a tightrope without a safety net, you can provide yourself with a margin of confidence by pursuing lifelong learning, being open and flexible, adapting to new ideas, and spending time with those who challenge your thinking. Be creative, seek innovative solutions, and supplement your past experience with a fresh perspective. Learn how to put your ideas into action, and be persistent, because achieving results takes time.

In addition, do your homework. Understand the business agenda, and close any gaps between what you are and what you could be. In other words, define your goals, and then create and implement a personal development plan.

Finally, demonstrate respect for others, and, trite as it sounds, apply the Golden Rule: doing unto others as you would have them do unto you. Why? Because achieving great results with great behavior helps your star rise.

Raise your star with exemplary behaviors like these:

- Finding the positive in negative situations
- Learning from the past
- Making time for others
- Understanding the culture, values, and beliefs of your organization

- Keeping things in perspective
- Maintaining your sense of humor
- Inspiring those around you to exceed expectations
- Consistently driving issues to closure

Once your star has risen, how do you ensure that it will be seen? Ask how your company identifies and rewards top performers. Inquire as to whether or not there is a "High Potential" category.

If you are searching for a new position or career, you should pursue an environment where the best employees are recognized and valued. It should be an organization that provides career growth, lifelong learning, and development opportunities. You also want meaningful work, an opportunity to contribute, and an environment that prizes new ideas and fresh perspectives. In addition, you deserve honest feedback and the opportunity to provide the same in return.

Finally, seek an organization that energizes and empowers you, encourages your good health, respects your point of view, and honors your performance. Organizations like this abound.

Action Steps to Develop Your Potential and Prepare for Greater Responsibility

- Learn to see the big picture. What are the priorities? What is the view from your boss's perspective? What are the issues that keep your CEO up at night?

- Know why your job was created, how it relates to your organization, and what opportunities it offers.

- Positively influence outcomes through your performance and achievements.

- Invest in your organization. Make decisions as if you owned the company.

- Determine which actions promise the most significant impact, and then pursue them with zeal.

Thanks to You, the Reader

Dear Colleague,

By applying the principles in this book, you can rev up, revitalize, or renew your career beginning anytime you choose, whatever your profession. Indeed, through lifelong learning and clear communication both with yourself and with others, you can create an environment that allows you to evolve to your highest level. What is that level? It is the one that maximizes your talent and expands your passion, speeds up growth, and brings great success. Ultimately, it is the point at which you step up and joyfully pursue the business of life. Thanks for reading.

With best wishes for success,

S. Gary Snodgrass